THE INTERNET PRIMER

Getting Started on Internet

Fritz J. Erickson
Millersville University of Pennsylvania

John A. Vonk
University of Northern Colorado

IRWIN
Chicago • Bogotá •Boston • Buenos Aires • Caracas
London • Madrid • Mexico City • Sydney • Toronto

Irwin Book Team

Publisher: *Tom Casson*
Sponsoring editor: *Garrett Glanz*
Developmental editor: *Kristin Hepburn*
Associate marketing manger: *Michelle Hudson*
Project editor: *Jane Lightell*
Production supervisor: *Dina L. Genovese*
Assistant manger, graphics: *Charlene R. Perez*
Senior designer: *Heidi J. Baughman*
Printer: *Malloy Lithographing, Inc.*

ISBN 0-256-23801-4

Printed in the United States of America
2 3 4 5 6 7 8 9 0 ML 3 2 1 0 9 8 7 6

Preface

If you look in the computer section in a bookstore, you will see a number of books on how to use the Internet. Many of these books are filled with technical jargon and loaded with acronyms such as TCP/IP, SLIP, PPP, http, DNS, VT100, and X.400. The size of the books and the large number of abbreviations suggest that learning to use the Internet is a complicated processes. Not so. Learning to use the Internet is not very difficult if you have a little guidance. On the other hand, learning to use the Internet can be difficult if you limit yourself to a trial-and-error approach.

Our goal is to show you how to access and use some of the Internet's more common features. You will not be an Internet expert. Instead you will have just enough knowledge to get started. For those wanting more, try *Effective Internet*. As a companion to *Modern Microcomputers*, *Effective Internet* provides you with a much broader examination of the Internet features and uses. It takes you step-by-step through the most critical elements of using the Internet.

Hi Mom

Table of Contents

Chapter 1
Welcome to Internet

Welcome

You have heard the hype. "The Internet can provide answers for the problems that face humanity." "You do not have to leave your home to go to work because, with the Internet, you have access to all the world's information." "You can find a date, develop a relationship, even get married on the Internet." "You don't have to go to college; an Internet college can come to you." "With the Internet's instant communications you will never need paper or the postal service again."

You have also heard the naysayers. "The Internet teaches terrorists how to build bombs, provides pedophiles with access to unsuspecting children, and allows extremists to spread their messages of hate." "It's just computer sex." "The Internet will doom us to a life of sitting in front of little computer screens and turn the creative human mind to bits and bytes."

Most of us who use the Internet hate the hype and fear the naysayers, but we know, at least in part, that both are right to some extent. Yes, the Internet offers a great potential to communicate. Yes, you can meet people, carry on conversations, have social gatherings, and even meet the wrong people on Internet. You can send notes to friends all over the world almost instantaneously. But the Internet is not a magical and mystical system. It is no different from any other technological advance, you get the good with the bad. Most think that the good far outweighs the bad.

What Is Internet?

This is not an easy question to answer. The Internet means different things to different people. Some view the Internet as a system of telephone wires, fiber optics, satellite links, and other attachments that allow computers to connect. Others view the Internet as a tool for sending electronic mail or as a system for accessing information sources all over the world.

Figure 1-1   Surfing the Web (as it is popularly known) is very easy with browsers such as Netscape

The "net" in Internet refers to network. A network is a collection of computers linked together to achieve some common goal. In most cases, networks allow users to share information. In business, networks enable one computer to send messages or get information from another computer. For example, a business may have a network that allows the sales department to access inventory files, new product announcements, and demonstrations of services. In schools, networks allow teachers to access student records, library catalog listings, and class registrations. The Internet is no different from any other network, except it is bigger.

The Internet is a network of networks. It is a series of networks that use very precise rules that allow any user to connect to and use any available network or computer connected to the Internet. When you use any computer connected to the Internet you have access to many other connected computers. In other words, connecting to the Internet means connecting to tens of thousands of other networks, millions of individual computers, and tens of millions of other computer users.

The Internet Structure

Internet is also a communication system that involves physical connections (usually telephone lines, direct wires, fiber optics, satellite transmissions, etc.) that link one computer network to another. To make this connection work, the Internet uses a standard of communication (called a protocol) that enables one computer network to "speak" to another. During the 1980's a new communication language, or protocol, emerged called Transmission Control Protocol/Internet Protocol (TCP/IP) that evolved into a communication standard for the Internet. In short, any computer network can communicate with any other computer network via the Internet as long as they use the TCP/IP standard protocol.

Addresses

Another important factor that makes the Internet possible is an agreed upon standard of addresses. Addresses on the Internet are, in many ways, similar to home addresses. Every network and every computer user must have a unique address. Without this address, information cannot be routed to its destination. The structure of Internet addresses is, therefore, very important.

The addressing system for Internet is actually quite easy because of a process called Domain Name System (DNS). Actual Internet addresses are numerical and are called IP Addresses (for example, 128.16.4.23). However, most users never see or use IP Address directly because DNS provides a more meaningful and easier-to-remember name. It all happens in the background. The host computer converts a DNS to an IP Address so you don't need to know the numbers.

A DNS name is made up of a domain and one or more subdomains. For example, *marauder.millersv.edu* uses the domain *edu* (educational institution) and has two subdomains, *millersv* and *marauder*. The first subdomain is the name of the network (*millersv*). The second subdomain, *marauder*, is the name of the computer system. If you read this address backwards, it is the educational institution Millersville University, using the Marauder computer. There can be more than two subdomains, and very often there are four or more. The key point is that the address is specific to a computer.

Domains
.com	commercial
.edu	educational
.gov	governmental
.mil	military
.org	organization
.net	network resources

Because the Internet is worldwide, some addresses indicate the country in addition to a domain. For example, a DNS ending with .ca is Canada and .uk is the United Kingdom.

In addition to identifying and locating a specific computer system through the Internet, it is also important to identify specific individuals who have valid accounts on a specific computer. This is the reason for the @ (at) symbol. For example, *ferickso@marauder.millersv.edu* indicates a specific individual at (@) the Marauder computer at Millersville University, which is an educational institution. Of the millions of people using Internet, no two have the exact same address.

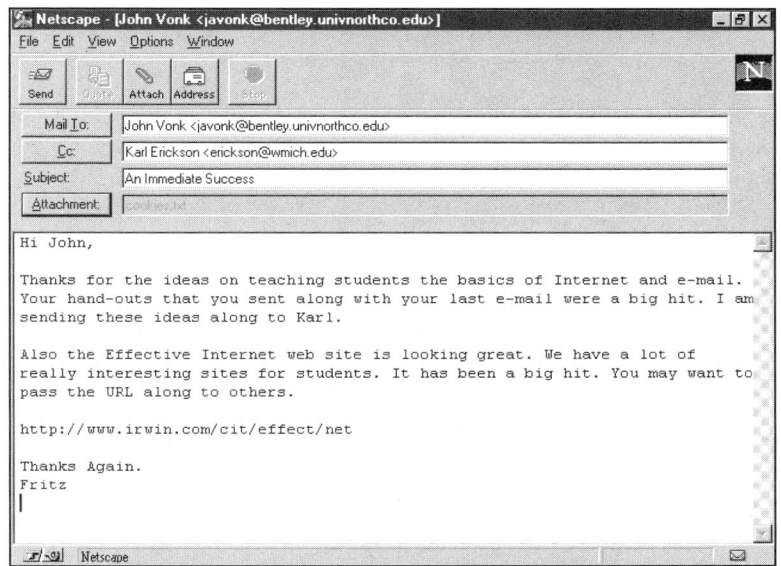

Figure 1-2   Electronic mail (e-mail) on the Internet is quickly becoming a common method for communicating. All you need to send mail is Internet access and the other person's address.

Points of Access

How and where you connect determines how you can use the Internet. The interface (how the Internet appears to you) can differ. Some interfaces are graphical while others are character-based (UNIX). This diversity poses a bit of a problem. What you can do is fairly standard, but how you do it is not. A very few providers (usually colleges and universities) provide a text only system. This is because colleges and universities provided the early backbone of the Internet before graphical interfaces were popular. Most providers, including most colleges and universities, allow you to use a graphical interface written for Microsoft Windows® (or Macintosh®) to access the Internet. With graphical software, you can use the point-and-click features of a mouse with pull-down menus and all of the advantages of Windows (or Mac).

The big advantage of a graphical interface is that you can view graphics (pictures) directly. You can also access and use sounds, video clips, and other multimedia information directly. Character-based systems provide the same access as graphical systems but do not allow you to view graphics directly. With character-based systems, you must use character-based, or command-driven software.

Within the basic framework of character-based and graphical interfaces, there are many different programs for accessing and using the Internet. One of the most critical pieces of software is called a Web browser (or simply a browser). Browsers allow you to access the World Wide Web — one of the most popular features of the Internet. There are many graphical browsers available (such as Netscape, Mosaic) including those specialized browsers from Internet providers (CompuServe®, America On-line®, Microsoft Network®, etc.). They all work in a similar fashion, so learning to use one makes it easy to learn to use any other. There are also character-based (UNIX) browsers. The way these systems operate depends, in large part, on the provider. Character-based systems differ, yet the basic functions remain the same.

Internet Ethics

No matter how you connect to the Internet, there are some rules, some common courtesies, and a few words of caution.

First, a few words of caution. Internet is public. Any information you put on the Internet will be available to millions of people. If you disseminate personal information, you do so at your own risk. Use common sense. Be especially careful about giving out your credit card number, home phone number, or even your personal address. Others may get it.

Caution is especially important for children. As in any public place, children need to be taught that the vast majority of people are decent, honorable, and trustworthy. The problem is, there area few who are not. Children should be taught never to give any personal information to Internet strangers.

Within these cautions, it is important to understand the culture of the Internet. Internet users are committed to free and open access. Freedom is the cornerstone of the Internet. Many users believe they should be able to access, retrieve, and post any information. Of course, with this freedom goes the responsibility not to post information that is harmful, destructive, and threatening. If you violate these unwritten rules, there can be consequences including Internet users flooding your e-mail account with undesirable messages.

Here are a few don'ts.

> Don't post hate or threatening files or mail.
> Don't post obscene files in public places.
> Don't ask for personal information.
> Don't damage files.
> Don't spread viruses.
> Don't tie up a connection with excessive game playing.
> Don't access computers and files unless you have permission.

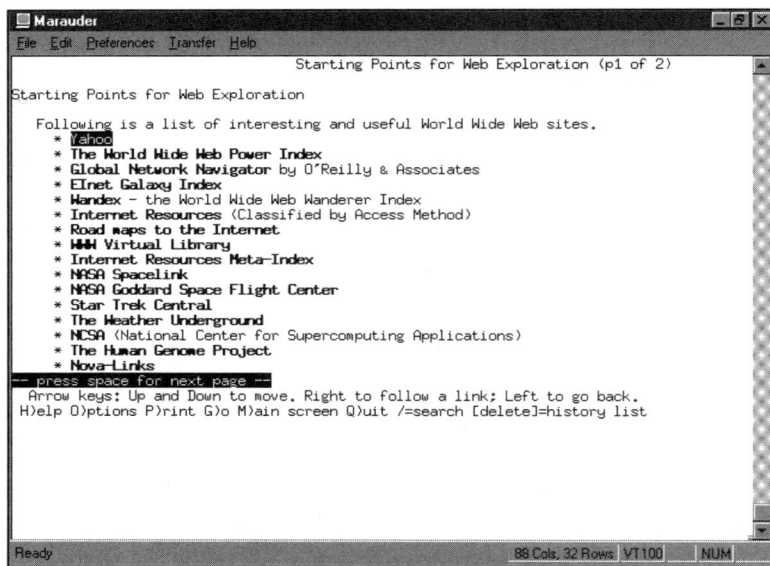

Figure 1-3   You don't need a graphical interface to access a wealth of information on the Internet.

A Quick Primer

Using the Internet involves using one of several services. Each of these services provides a different procedure for using the Internet. This guide gives you an opportunity to explore and use each service. Here is what they allow you to do.

E-mail

Electronic mail is considered by many to be the cornerstone of Internet. It is what Internet users employ to communicate with other Internet users. As described earlier, e-mail can work because every user has a unique address based on a username. Most Internet e-mail systems allow you to create mailing lists. From these lists you can send mail to millions of users (depending on the capability of the software you are using). How you use e-mail will depend on which e-mail software you have available.

World Wide Web (WWW)

The World Wide Web (commonly called the Web) has become one of the most popular Internet services because it allows both character-based and graphical access depending on your software tools and your service provider. With the World Wide Web, you can locate information provided by others, or you can establish your own Internet location. A Web location is called a Web page, Web site, or home page. Every Web page has a specific address, called a URL (Uniform Resource Locator), that looks something like *http:\\www.irwin.com/cit/net*. The *http* stands for HyperText Transfer Protocol, the rest is the address.

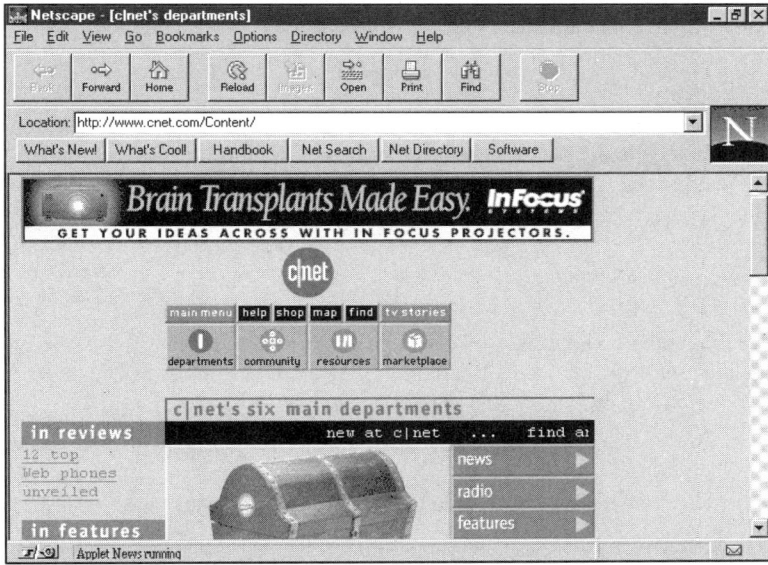

Figure 1-4   With the Web (as it is commonly called), you can go almost anywhere by knowing just the http address.

Netscape, Lynx, and other Web Tools

The World Wide Web is made up of documents created with a special language called the HyperText Markup Language (HTML). HyperText Markup Language allows the full use of hypermedia including text, images, graphics, sounds, and other types of multimedia. Because HTML is a special language, it requires special software to access the Web. Web browsers are designed to read and interpret HTML documents. Netscape is one of several full-featured, graphical browsers that allow you to use color graphics, a mouse, and all of the features common to Microsoft Windows and Macintosh. There are also character-based versions of this software. Lynx is a popular character-based (UNIX) browser that allows you to view only the text portions of Web pages and of other resources created with HTML. Other browsers are specific to providers or services such as CompuServe or the Microsoft Network.

Gopher

Gopher is a navigational tool that uses a system of standardized menus for navigating among various computers on the Internet. By linking several gophers together on a simple menu, you can move through the Internet and locate a wealth of information. One of the nice features of a gopher is that it is very easy to use. Because the structure of gophers is standardized, after you enter Internet through a gopher, you simply follow a maze of menus to browse for information.

Both gopher and the World Wide Web are tools for locating and displaying information on the Internet. The World Wide Web however is much more flexible. Gophers force you to move through the Internet using a series of menus, but the Web allows you to go directly to any home page you desire. In fact, you can even use the a Web browser and the Web to access a gopher or any menu within a gopher by using the specific gopher site's URL.

Veronica

There are tens of thousands of gophers available on the Internet. This makes it often difficult to locate the gopher you want for specific information. Veronica is a search tool and database for gophers. You can use Veronica to locate a specific gopher or locate gophers that contain information on specific search criteria.

Telnet

Telnet allows you to connect to any host computer on the Internet as if you were directly connected. For example, if you want to connect to the University of Michigan's computer, you need the URL for that computer and permission to use the system. When you telnet (the term telnet can be used as a verb) to another remote computer, your computer operates as if you were sitting in a computer lab for that computer. Usually, you need a password to access and use the remote.

FTP

File Transfer Protocol (ftp) allows you to send files and receive files from other computers connected through the Internet. These files include data files and program files (called binary files). With ftp you have access to millions of files, both public and private. Of course, with private files you will need access privileges. However, there are many public files available through open public ftp sites. These are commonly known as anonymous ftp sites. By using ftp you can obtain copies of software, documents, games, almost anything.

FAQ

Frequently Asked Questions (FAQ) are special files that contain common questions and answers about Internet use. FAQs answer common questions so users do not need to ask the same questions over and over. FAQs are usually available through Web browsers, ftp, gophers, and Usenet. FAQs are also frequently included in mailing lists.

Usenet

Usenet has been called the world's largest bulletin board because it is a public place where users can read and post messages. Actually there are thousands of Usenets on a variety of topics. To access and read information posted on a Usenet you need special software called a news reader. As with every other type of software for accessing and using Internet resources, there are a variety of news readers available both in graphical and character-based form.

Listserv

Listservs are automated mailing lists. When you join a listserv, any mail sent to the listserv will also be sent to you. Also, any mail you send to the listserv will be sent to all other members. While listservs are very popular and cover thousands of topics, there is a bit of a danger. If you join a listserv with thousands of active members, you may receive several hundred e-mail messages a day.

Chapter 2
World Wide Web and Gopher

What Is the Web?

The World Wide Web (WWW), or, as it is commonly called, "the Web", has quickly become the most popular way to access and use the Internet. The reason is simple. The Web allows full, high-quality color graphics and sound that make it an ideal multimedia tool.

Figure 2-1   The World Wide Web allows the full use of text, graphics, sound, animation, and video. It is a powerful multimedia tool.

The World Wide Web was initiated by the European Laboratory for Particle Physics as a means for linking objects (text, graphics, sound, etc.). By using HyperText Markup Language (HTML), anyone can create documents consisting of several objects for inclusion on the Web. Most documents created by users with HTML are called Web pages.

All Web pages are identified by a specific address called a Uniform Resource Locator (URL). A URL identifies the protocol for transferring data over the Internet. Web pages use the HyperText Transfer Protocol (HTTP). However, you can also use URLs to access nearly all resources on the Internet including gophers, ftp, telnet, and so on. In short, if you know a URL, you can go directly to that location without having to search through a series of menus.

Using a Browser

One of the requirements for using the Web is that you must have a browser. A browser is software that supports both the HyperText Transfer Protocol (http) and the HyperText Markup Language (HTML) including Netscape, Lynx, Mosaic, Cello, and many others. Some browsers are dedicated to specific on-line services such as CompuServe or Microsoft Network.

Lynx is a popular character-based (UNIX) browser that can be used to access all available information on the Web. However, being character-based, Lynx cannot directly display graphics or use sounds. For example, graphic objects appear as the word `[Image]` on Lynx. You can, however, download these objects and use other software to view them.

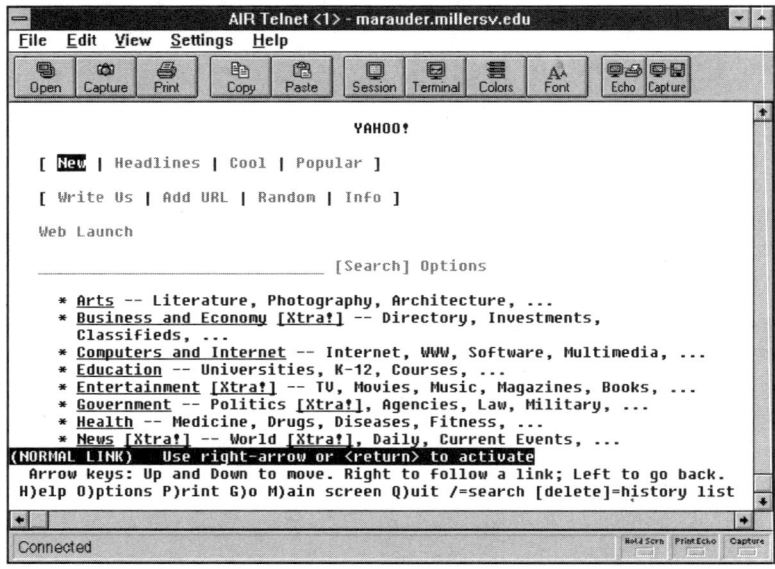

Figure 2-2   With Lynx,you must use arrow keys to navigate through various options and selections on a Web page.

Netscape and other graphic browsers display images as buttons, icons, or the actual image. With Netscape you can use a mouse to access these objects, display graphics directly, and take full advantage of HTML. In addition, Netscape and most other graphical browsers, provide specific features that make accessing and using the Web even easier. One common feature allows you to create a system for storing your favorite locations within the Web. For example, with Netscape you can create bookmarks. Items in your bookmark list can be accessed quickly and directly by clicking the mouse button on your list.

A Quick Guide to Netscape

Of course Netscape is not the only browser to take full advantage of the graphic characteristics of the Web. However, it is one of the most popular. Even if you use a different browser, learning the basics of Netscape will make learning to use any of the other browsers easier.

In most cases, the first step in using Netscape (after you have made the connection) is to activate an HTML document identified through its URL. Many colleges and universities, service providers, or on-line services automatically display a home page that is a helpful starting point. If you have a home page displayed, you should see the location of the home page listed next to Location: and the name of the current Web page appears in the title bar.

Of course, the Location: is most critical because it identifies the location of a home page or other document. With this text box you can enter any valid URL (including http, gopher, and ftp) you desire. Pressing enter after entering a valid location will cause the document or Web page to appear. The real trick to using Netscape is knowing the location of information that you wish to access.

All HTML documents you locate on the Web appear in Netscape's document view window. When you access an HTML document, Netscape interprets the document and then displays the results of the document including any graphics, sounds, animations, video, and, of course, text. Text will appear in the format (font, size, and style) set forth in the HTML document. Interpreting a document is why browsers are required to use the Web.

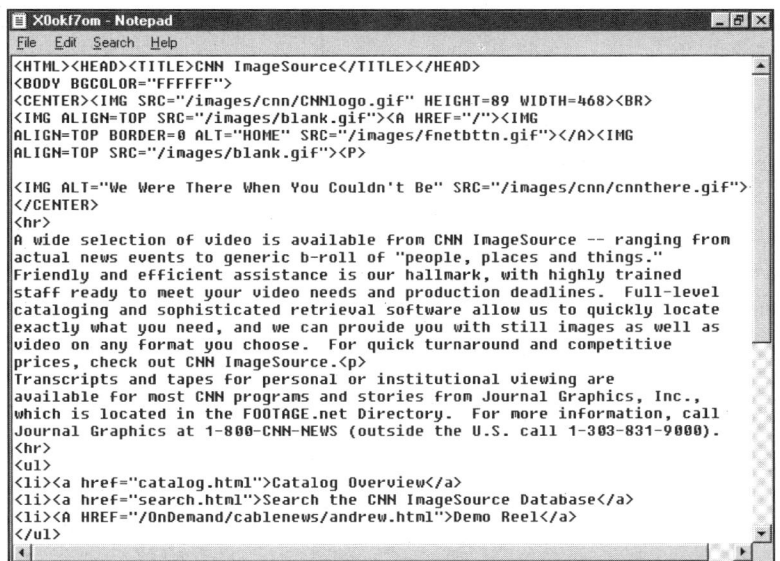

Figure 2-3 Here is the HTML source document from Fig 2-1. Netscape interprets the HTML code and displays high quality graphics, audio and video files.

When you make a connection to an HTML document, the Netscape icon shows comets racing toward earth indicating that Netscape has sent forth a request to locate, load, and interpret a document. You can stop the locate, load, and interpret process at any time by clicking on the Stop button.

At the bottom of the screen is Netscape's status bar (sometimes called the status line). The status bar displays any link to a URL address. For example, if you point at an icon in the document view window, the link to that object is another URL. The status bar also displays the process of downloading and interpreting. When you are downloading a graphic, the size of the graphic and the completion rate appear. There may be times that you do not want to wait for a large graphic to download. This information helps you decide when to click on the Stop button.

Another important feature of Netscape are the navigation buttons. Navigation buttons assist you in locating various URLs. The first of these navigation buttons are the arrow buttons. In some versions of Netscape, these are the Forward and Back buttons. The Back button is used to return to the previous page. For example, if you access a URL and then select a button from the document view window, a second URL appears. Clicking on the Back button returns you the previous URL. If you are surfing the net (moving from one page to another), the Back button will allow you to back track through each page you have entered. The Forward button works the same as the Back button only in reverse. It sends you forward through previously selected pages up to the last page you accessed.

The Open button, or the Open Location command from the File menu, is very useful. If you find a URL that you want, you can type the URL address into the Open Location box and connect directly to that URL. Many users find it easier to enter a URL directly next to Location:. At any point you can delete the existing URL and type a new one.

Bookmarks is a very useful feature. With Bookmarks you can store the URL of your favorite locations on the Web. The more you surf the net, the more interesting places you will find. If you do not remember a URL, you will have a difficult time returning to it. By using bookmarks you can store and recall various locations on the Web.

History is another useful navigational tool because it keeps track of where you have been on the Web. History is available through the Window menu in Netscape. By examining History you can quickly return to any URL previously entered.

These are just a few of the tools common to most versions of Netscape and other graphics-based browsers. Netscape is very easy to use and for the most part intuitive. If you get stuck when you begin to use Netscape, there is a Help option. Help provides you with access to the Netcom server and provides you with a detailed user manual. It does not provide you with on-line help as is the case with most Microsoft Windows applications.

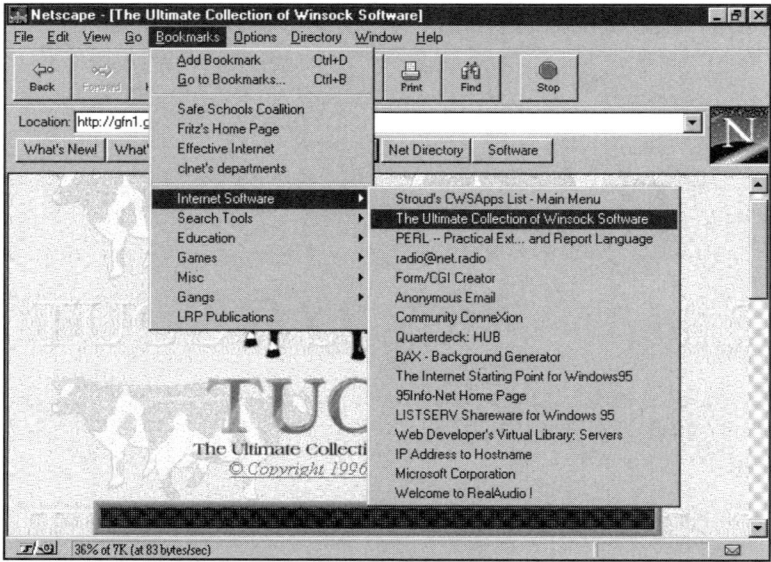

Figure 2-4   Bookmarks make it easy to quickly move to various sites
                        throughout the Web.

A Quick Guide to Lynx

As mentioned, Lynx is a character-based browser for the Web. It was developed at the University of Kansas as a means for accessing the Web through UNIX, VMS, and DOS (all primarily character-based systems). You can access any URL you wish through Lynx, but you will not see any graphics, animations, or videos, or hear any sounds.

The key feature of Lynx is the keyboard command menu located at the bottom of the screen. This menu lists some of the more common Lynx commands and provides access to other Lynx commands. To access a URL, you must use the G)o command. This will allow you to enter any valid URL (such as *http:\\www.irwin.com/cit/effect/net*).

After a document appears on your screen, the most common way of navigating through it is with arrow keys. The up and down arrow keys allow you to move one line. Each link is typically identified by boldfaced text. The left and right arrow keys allow you to move a page at a time. The following is a list of common Lynx commands and their uses.

Lynx Commands

Key	Outcome
Up Arrow	Back one link
Down Arrow	Forward one link
Left Arrow	Back one page
Right Arrow	Forward one page
-	Back one screen
+	Forward one screen
space bar	Forward one screen
7 (number pad)	Top of current page

1 (number pad)	Bottom of current page
/	Search string
\	View HTML format page
backspace	History list
delete	History list
?	Help
a	Create bookmark
b	Top of current page
c	Send comments to page owner
d	Download current page
e	Edit current page
g	Go to a URL
i	Web index
m	Return to first page
n	Search for keyword
o	Options menu
p	Print, save, or send to electronic mail address
q	Quit Lynx
r	Remove bookmark
s	Search string
u	Previous document
v	Access bookmark list
z	Abort

Using Yahoo and Other Search Tools

The Web is only as useful as the information you find. If you cannot locate useful pages, the Web will be of little value. The trick, then, is to find pages with information you want. To do this there are a variety of search tools. One of the most popular tools is called Yahoo. However, there are others including the Webcrawler, Excite, Lycos, and more. All of these tools are very useful when searching for specific information on the Web.

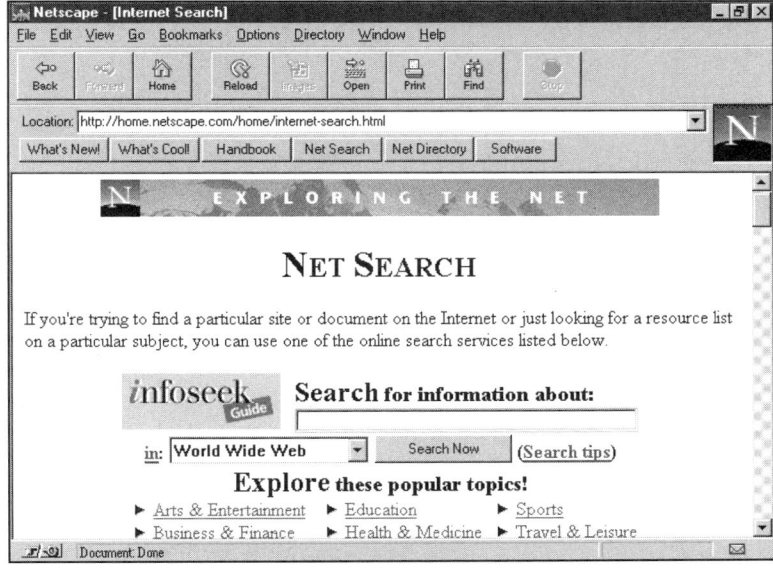

Figure 2-5   Netscape provides you direct access to a variety of search tools.

Yahoo, and other search tools, are popular because they allow keyword searching. When you access Yahoo you have the option of entering one or more keywords then clicking on the Search button. Clicking on Search returns a list of all sites that match the keyword. From this list you can then select the links that you desire.

Another feature that is most useful in Yahoo are the predefined categories. Instead of searching for specific keywords you can move through the various categories to search for interesting and informative sites. For example, you can select the category Arts. From this you will receive a listing of information on the Arts ranging from Architecture to Literature, from Museums to Events, and almost every other topic related to the Arts.

The Web also provides several other searching procedures. WAIS is actually a series of indexed databases that identify the location of documents based on keyword searches. Therefore, if you are looking for information on a particular topic WAIS is an ideal search tool. One feature that makes WAIS so popular is that most searches are frequently transparent. That is, a search is conducted and the user doesn't even notice a search is occurring. Many times when you select a search process from a page, you are actually performing a WAIS search.

To perform a WAIS search, you must access a page that has searching capability, enter a keyword, then press Enter to initiate the search. The results of the search appear as a list of documents by title along with a score. A score of 1000 means the keyword was fully identified. A score of 100 means that the keyword is borderline. You can go to any of the documents by selecting a document from the list.

There are other search procedures and tools. Most of these are actual pages developed as a service for Web users. The Lycos, Excite, and the Webcrawler are common examples. These search tools work much like Yahoo for searching for different Web pages. The search process is similar. All you need to do is access the search tool Web page and then complete the form. The results of the search will quickly appear.

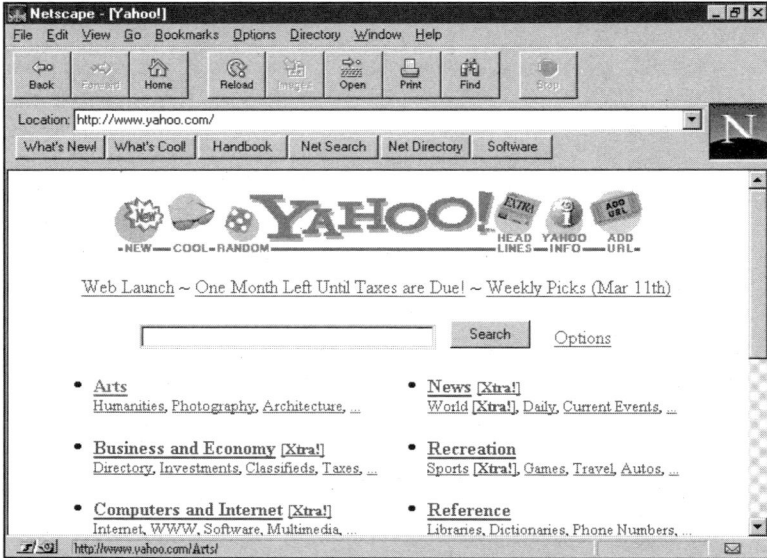

Figure 2-6   Yahoo is a popular subject-oriented directory that provides access to a variety of pages.

A Quick Tour of the Web

Now that you have some idea of how to use a browser and search tools, it is time to begin examining some interesting information on the Web. This guided tour is intended to give you a quick sample of some of the kinds of information available on the Web. Keep in mind that there is a tremendous amount of information available on the Internet and this is only a brief introduction.

Surfing the Web can be a lot of fun. There is so much information out on the Web that just exploring can lead to information that is fascinating and very useful. To begin surfing you need a starting point. A good starting point is a search tool such as Yahoo. Yahoo is located at *http://www.yahoo.com*. Yahoo is also provided as a link on several other Web pages.

When you go to Yahoo a list of categories appears. From this list of categories you can select any topic you like, such as Entertainment. Selecting Entertainment produces another page with a list of entertainment topics. From this list you can select Movies and get information on current movie releases. You can, of course, select other entertainment topics.

The strategy with Yahoo and other search tools is to remember where you have been. This is where the History command from the Windows menu in Netscape can be very useful. When you find a page that you would like to return to, you can do so by using History. If it is a page that you want for future reference, it is a good idea to keep the URL for that page as a bookmark or at the very least write the URL in your own personal Web book. By the way, keeping a Web book can save you hours trying to retrace your steps to find that page you liked so much.

The following list is a small sampling of some places to explore. Learning to use the Web means spending time just looking around. A note of caution. The Web is changing daily. Some of these sites may have moved and use new URLs and some sites may have left the Web.

Some Places to Explore

Mother-of-all BBS
  http:///www.cs.colorado.edu/homes/mcbryan/public_html/bb/summary.html
Planet Earth Home Page
  http://white.nosc.mil/info.html
CyberNet
  http://cybersight.com/cgi-bin/cs/s?main.gmml
Meta-Index
  http://www.ncsa.uiuc.edu/SDG/Software/Mosaic/MetaIndex.html
Yahoo
  http://www.yahoo.com/
Information Services
  http://www.rpi.edu/Internet/Guides/decemj/internet-cmc.html
ElNet's Galaxy UourcesRL
  http://www.einet.net/galaxy.html
Yanoff's List
  http://www.uwm.edu/MNirror/inet.services.html
O'Reilly's Whole Internet Catalog
  http://www.ora.com
CERN's Virtual Library
  http://infor.cern.ch/hypertext/DataSources/bySubject/Overview.html
Downtown Anywhere
  http://www.awa.com
The OTIS Project
  http://sunsite.unc.edu/otis/otis.html
The Louvre
  http://mistral.enst.fr/-pioch/lourve/
World Wide Web Sports
  http://tns-www.lcs.mit.edu/cgi-gin/sports

Thomas Jefferson High School for Science and Technology
> http://boom.tjhsst.edu

The Whole Frog Project
> http://george.lbl.gov/ITG.hm.pg.docs

Games
> http://wcl-rs.bham.ac.uk/GamesDomain.

What Is a Gopher?

Gopher is a menuing system designed to provide a standardized structure for accessing a wide variety of Internet services. It is an information browser developed by the University of Minnesota, who are also known as the Golden Gophers. By using a series of menus, it is possible to navigate among various computers, gain access to numerous databases, locate files (text, graphics, audio, software, etc.), and a whole lot more. Prior to the development of the World Wide Web, gophers provided the most common method for navigating the Internet. Today, gophers still provide a quick and easy method for locating information and can be accessed through the Web.

When you start a gopher session, you begin by accessing an initial menu. Normally, this menu reflects information that is available on your home computer. For example, if you connect to a gopher through a college or university, you will probably access your college or university gopher. From this gopher menu, you then can begin to branch out to other menus and other gophers. Gopher is a menu character-based navigational tool. When you select a menu option, it normally leads you to another gopher menu.

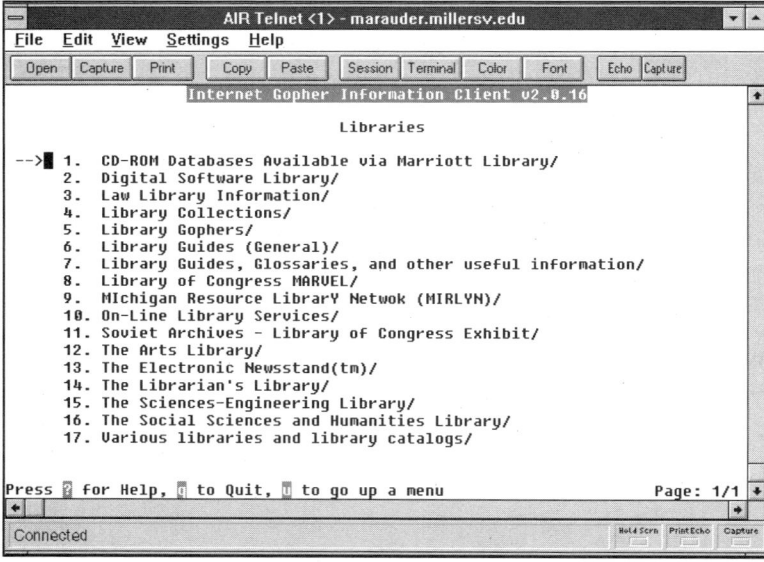

Figure 2-7   Using a standardized menuing system, gophers provide one of the easiest ways to access and locate information on Internet.

A Quick Tour of Gopher

As with other Internet resources, the way you start a gopher session is determined by your host computer. Some computer systems allow you to access a gopher through a simple menu. Other systems require you to type **gopher** at a prompt. You can also access a gopher through a URL on the Web or use dedicated gopher software. Either way, when you start a gopher session, you will see an initial, or top, gopher menu.

One of the advantages of using the Web is all resources on the Internet have a unique URL. This includes gophers. The difference between accessing a Web page and a gopher is that Web page URL's begins with http:, while gopher URL's begin with gopher:. For example, the Online Book Initiative gopher uses the URL gopher://gopher.std.com:70/11/obi. Of course, this means you need to know the gopher address to get to this location.

One of the strengths of using a gopher is its simplicity. Once you get a gopher menu, navigating is accomplished by selecting menu options. Typically, you can either type the number corresponding to the option you wish to select, or you can use the up and down arrow keys to highlight your choices, then press Enter.

If you access a gopher through UNIX, menu options that end with either a right arrow or a home slash (/) indicate that the option produces another menu. Options that end with a period (.) are files. Options that end with a question mark (?) are indexed directories. If you access a gopher through Netscape, other Web browsers, or through specific Windows or Mac based gopher software documents or files are identified with one icon and folders with another.

You do have a few commands to help you navigate through gopher menus. From UNIX, normally, you can get help (?), quit (q), and go up one menu (u). When you select and display a file, there are several other menu options including exit (u), page up (b), and page down (Spacebar). From Netscape or other browsers or specific gopher software you can navigate by clicking the mouse button and scrolling in the same fashion you would use any other Windows or Mac based software.

Gopher Features

Downloading
Since Gopher is a character-based system, you can display basic text files directly on your computer screen but you cannot display formatted text files (those generated by a word processor), graphics, or sounds. To use these files you must download the file to your host computer. From there you may download the file to your personal computer. Text files generally refer to ASCII or unformatted files. All other types of files are referred to as binary files which are the files, you need to download to use.

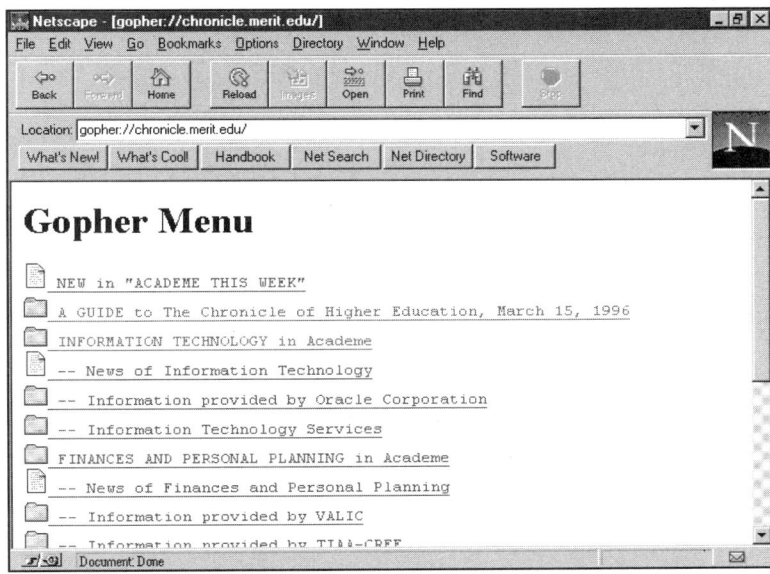

Figure 2-8   With Netscape, or any other Web browser, enter the gopher URL to go directly to a gopher site.

To download a file, you need to locate the download command. This will normally cause a menu to appear allowing you to select a particular file transfer protocol. It does not matter which protocol you select, as long as your system or communication software supports it. Kermit is very popular with mini or mainframe computers. Zmodem is popular with personal computers. You need to check your system to determine which protocol to use.

Bookmarks

When you use a gopher, you will spend a lot of time moving from one menu to the next. It is very common for users to get lost. If you simply quit to leave the gopher it becomes difficult to return to that same exact spot. If you find something you really like, it is a good idea to have a bookmark for that location so you can return quickly. Depending on the software you are using, there is almost always a bookmark command.

Chapter 3
Electronic Mail

What Is E-Mail?

Electronic mail (e-mail) is a method of composing, editing, sending, and receiving messages (mail) electronically. It is really not much different from writing a letter and using the post office to mail the letter. E-mail is just faster and easier.

E-mail was one of the first applications on Internet. In fact, e-mail remains one of the primary reasons there are so many Internet users. Internet gained wide acceptance, in large part, because it provided an easy system for sending messages, almost instantly, from one computer to another.

E-mail systems consist of two programs — user agents and mail delivery systems. You interact with a user agent as a means of generating, sending, and receiving mail. The mail delivery system routes your mail to its intended destination. With Internet, mail is delivered within the system by a program called Simple Mail Transport Protocol (SMTP). In most cases you will never need to be concerned with SMTP (although it is a good idea to know that it exists). Most users interact with electronic mail through the user agent. Therefore, the term e-mail usually refers to the user agent.

E-Mail Structure

E-mail is made up of two very important components — header lines and mail body. Header lines tell the computer where to send the mail. Typically, there are five header lines: To:, CC:, From:, Date:, and Subject:. To: is very important because it is where you address e-mail. The To: determines who gets the mail. It must contain the valid address of a user. If you do not include a valid address, the mail cannot be routed. CC: allows you to send a copy of the message to one or more other users. This line must also include a valid user address. Both To: and CC: are called destination header lines because they identify where the message is going. From: is the sender (you). Date: is normally generated automatically to identify when the message was sent. Finally, Subject: tells the recipient what the mail is about. The Subject: will appear in the recipient's list of mail. From:, Date:, and Subject: are referred to as originator header lines.

The mail body is the message you create. With most e-mail systems you have variety of tools that simplify the writing process, including full editing capabilities and spell checking.

Addressing

The most critical element of an e-mail message is the address. If you want to send e-mail to someone, you must know his or her unique Internet address. If you do not address your mail correctly, it cannot be delivered. There is no room for error. If you miss someone's address by even one character, the mail will not go through.

In Chapter 1 we outlined the basic address structure. All e-mail consists of two primary components — host name and user name. These names are separated by the @ (at) sign. The host name is the unique name of the recipient's computer. For example, marauder.millersv.edu is a host name. The user name is the unique name on the host. For example, ferickso is a unique user name on the marauder.millersv.edu host. Therefore, the address ferickso@marauder.millersv.edu identifies one unique user on Internet.

Using E-Mail

As with World Wide Web browsers, several e-mail systems exist. Some are text based and others use a graphical interface. However, most work in much the same fashion. On the graphical side are programs such as Netscape Mail which is found within Netscape. This is accessible by selecting Netscape Mail from the Window menu. Since most e-mail programs work in much the same way, learning any e-mail package will make learning and using any other e-mail package more efficient. To give you an idea of how a typical e-mail system works, and the features that are commonly available, we will look at one of the most popular text (UNIX) based systems — Pine.

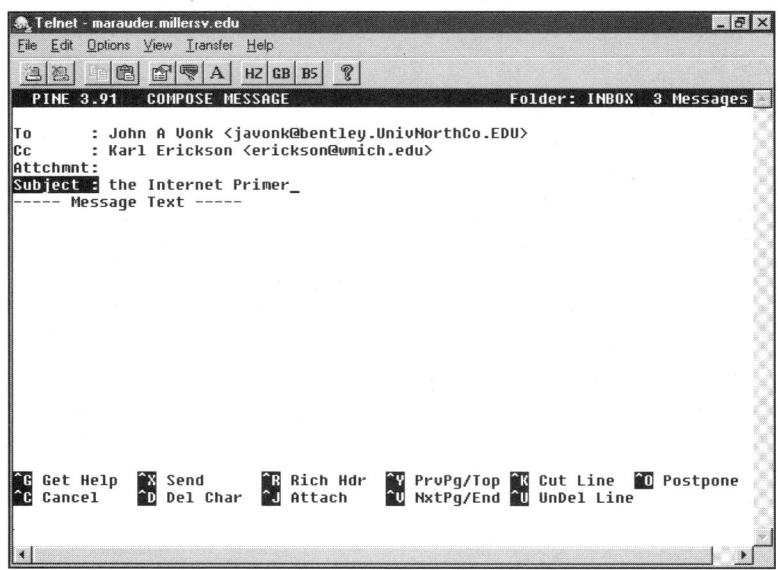

Figure 3-1   A header defines the location for sending electronic mail.

The way you access Pine (or other e-mail systems) will depend on your connection or your provider. Some systems require you to enter Pine from a prompt, while others let you launch Pine through menu options. Either way, once you launch Pine you are ready to send and receive e-mail.

The dominant feature of Pine is the main menu. The following is a list of Main Menu options.

?	HELP	Get help using Pine
C	COMPOSE	Compose and send a message
I	MAIL INDEX	Read mail in current folder
F	FOLDERS	Open a different mail folder
A	ADDRESSES	Update your address book
O	OTHER	Use other functions
Q	QUIT	Exit the Pine mail program

When you want to create and send a message you simply press C for COMPOSE. The compose screen consists of the header lines and mail body. You must enter the address for the person to whom you are sending the e-mail. Press Enter after typing the address; the cursor moves next to Cc:. Use Cc: to send a copy of the e-mail message to another person. Again, you must include a valid address. Attachment: allows you to send a file along with the message. The file must reside on the same machine that is running Pine. Therefore, if you want to attach a file and you are running from a dial-in facility, you must first send the file to your account on the host machine before attaching it to an e-mail message. This process varies, so it is a good idea to contact the host for proper attachment procedures. Finally, you may enter a subject which will appear on the recipient's list of incoming mail. Your address is sent automatically with your message.

After the header, you can type any message you desire. Apply the same rules of good taste to e-mail messages as you do to personal letters. When you complete your message you have several options (menu) at the bottom of the screen. The command ^X Send means you must hold down the Ctrl key then press X. You will be asked if you really want to send the mail. You may return to the main menu at any time without sending mail by using the ^C Cancel command.

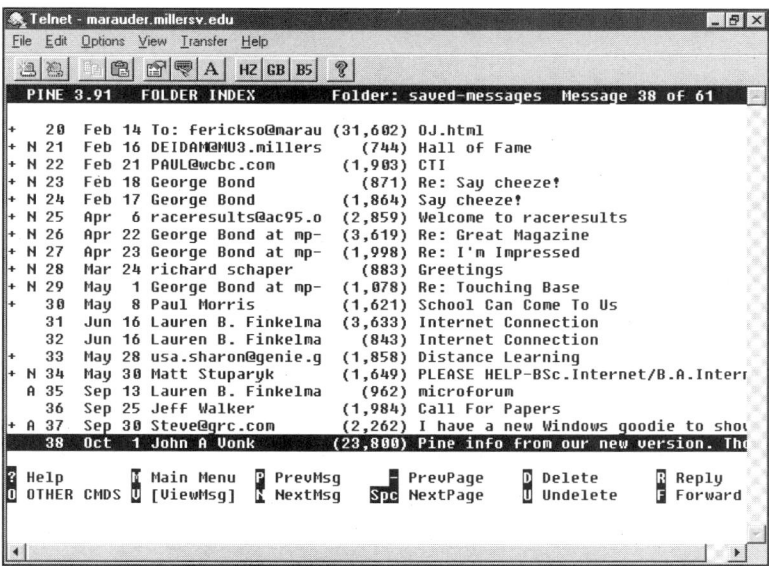

Figure 3-2   With Pine and other electronic mail software you can save mail for future references. Here is a sample listing of saved mail in Pine.

Whenever you create, send, or receive mail, it is stored in Pine within folders. A folder is simply a storage location. All incoming mail is held in the INBOX folder. The sent-mail folder holds mail you sent. Other folders, including saved-messages can help organize your e-mail. When you select I from the main menu for FOLDER LIST, a listing of all mail for the specified folder will appear. The INBOX folder is selected by default unless you first use the FOLDER LIST command (L) and select a different folder. From the FOLDER INDEX for INBOX, you will see a list of all mail organized by date of receipt. To read a piece of mail, arrow down to the desired mail and then press Enter.

All new mail is identified with the letter N preceding the mail date. After you read a piece of mail, you should move it out of the INBOX by using either the Delete command (^D) to erase the mail or the Save command (^S) to save the message in a specific folder. To get to the Save command, you need to select ^O for Other Commands and then select ^S.

Often when you read a message, you will want to reply immediately. This is accomplished with the Reply command (^R). By using Reply, the address of the sender is automatically inserted into the header lines; all you need to do is type a new message. If you want to send the message to another user use the Forward command (^F). At any point in a list of messages, you can return to the main menu by pressing ^M.

One of the most useful features of Pine is the ADDRESS BOOK command (A) from the main menu. This command allows you to store the names and address of other users. To add a new person to your personal address book, you must select the Add command (A). You will be prompted to enter a new full name, nickname, and e-mail address. If you use the nickname, then all you have to do to address an e-mail message to that person is type the nickname. For example, in the compose screen instead of typing ferickso@marauder.millersv.edu next to To:, you could type just Fritz — if you used that nickname. Nicknames make it much easier to remember and use e-mail addresses.

The Setup command from the main menu allows you to customize your system for a particular printer, set a new password, configure your system, and view any updates about Pine. In most cases, it is a good idea to set up your printer so you can directly print your e-mail messages.

These are only a few basic commands for using Pine. To learn more about the various features, use the Help command (?).

E-Mail Security

While it is unlikely that your mail will be read by an unintended user, do not ever assume that your mail is private. The delivery systems used to route your mail have human operators who have access to your mail. In most cases no one will ever care what you send, but your mail can be monitored. This is especially true with corporate e-mail.

E-mail can also be forged. Since the delivery systems are not designed to verify the contents of header lines, it is possible for someone to send mail to you under an false name. It is not all that difficult for a sophisticated user to send mail using another person's address. Keep this in mind, particularly if someone requests personal information. Children are especially vulnerable to forged, or inappropriate, mail and should be warned never to provide personal information such as a phone number, address, or age.

One of the problems that almost all regular e-mail users encounter is unwanted mail. This mail can range from "junk" mail much like you may receive through the postal service, to harassing mail. The more you make your e-mail address available, the more likely it is that you will receive unwanted mail. Before you give someone your e-mail address, make sure you want to receive mail from that source.

If you receive unwanted mail, you have several options. First, just delete the mail; this is the easiest option. If you continue to get unwanted mail from a particular source, send a reply asking to be removed from the mailing list. If this fails, send the system administrator a message indicating you have asked not to receive any mail from a particular source. These tips may or may not work. Unwanted mail is a price that users pay for the freedom of open access to Internet.

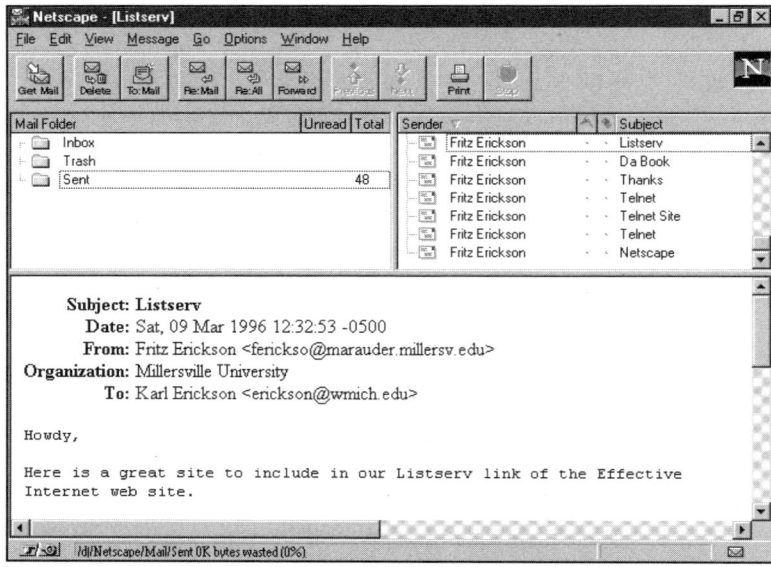

Figure 3-3   Netscape Mail offers many of the same features as Pine.

Chapter 4
Telnet and FTP

What Is Telnet?

Telnet is a system that allows you to connect to a remote computer on the Internet and then use that remote computer in much the same way you would if you were directly connected to it. In other words, you can use telnet to work directly on another computer. The key to using another computer is not so much telnet, as having a valid password and permission to use that computer. However, many systems make a portion of their system resources publicly available.

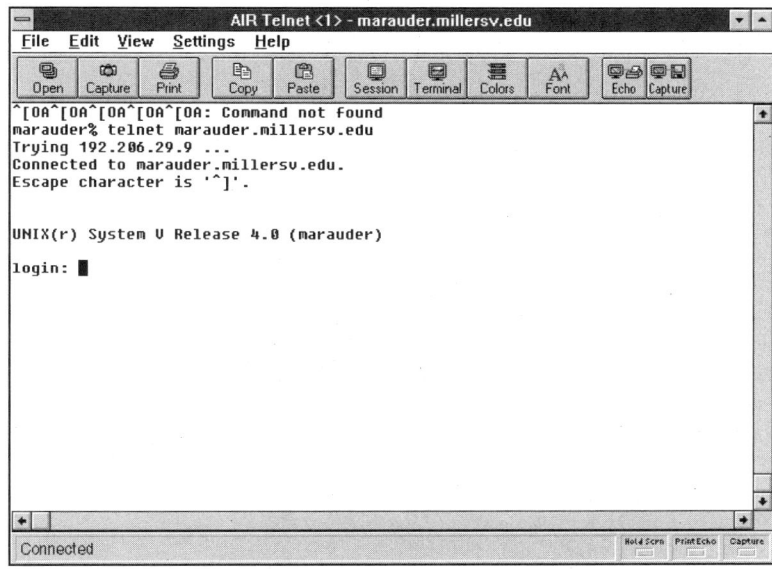

Figure 4-1   When you telnet to a remote computer, you are asked to log in and provide a password.

One big advantage of telnet is that you can be working a long distance away from your host computer and telnet to it and work as if you were on site. Another advantage is, if you are provided access, you can use computer resources that may not be available through your home or host computer. This allows you to take advantage of many more software applications, provides you with access to a wider range of files, and allows you to use high-speed sophisticated computers (that is, supercomputers) that may not be available at your host site. In order for telnet to work, both your access computer and the computer you want to telnet to must have the telnet software. This is normally not a problem, because telnet is a standard feature for most host computers and providers on the Internet.

A Quick Tour of Telnet

Telnet is one of the easiest resources to use on the Internet. Most of the operation of telnet is transparent. In fact, once you connect to another computer, telnet operations occur in the background leaving you free to concentrate on your applications.

The first step in using telnet, like other Internet resources, is to launch telnet. Some systems require you to enter the telnet command at a specific prompt. Other systems provide telnet as a menu choice. You can also use a URL to access a particular telnet site (telnet://address) if your browser software supports this feature. Either way, once you start telnet you need to identify the address of the telnet site. For example, the command *telnet marauder.millersv.edu* would start a telnet session and connect you to the *marauder.millersv.edu* computer.

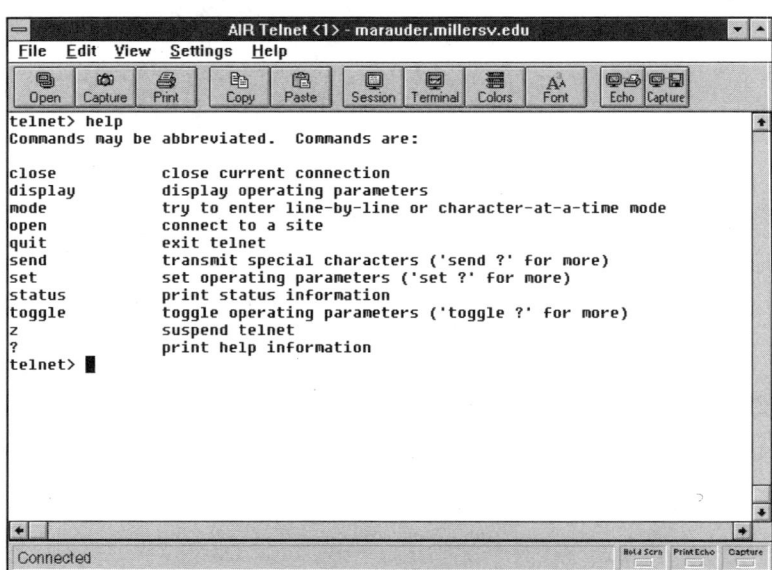

Figure 4-2   The telnet> prompt means you have activated the telnet
                      system and that telnet is waiting for a command.

The telnet site address follows the same addressing procedure as other Internet resources. For example, the telnet address for the Marauder computer at Millersville University is *marauder.millersv.edu*. This is often the same address used to identify a computer for e-mail. When you make a connection to a telnet site, a message similar to the following appears.

Connected to marauder.millersv.edu
Escape character is '^]'.

login:

The login prompt indicates you have a successful connection. At this point you use the same procedures for logging onto and using the computer as you would use if you were directly connected. After you complete the login process, the operations of telnet become transparent.

To leave or exit a telnet session, you normally use the standard exiting procedures used by the computer to which you are now connected. After you exit, you return either to your host system menu or command prompt. In some cases, you may return to a telnet> prompt. If you wish to leave telnet, use the quit command.

When you get the login screen for a telnet session, an escape character is identified. Entering the escape character causes the telnet> prompt from your host computer to appear, allowing you to use any available telnet command. It is important to take note of the escape character designated in the login screen. Different systems use different escape characters. Returning to the telnet> prompt provides you with access to a variety of telnet commands.

File Transfer Protocol (ftp)

The file transfer protocol (ftp) allows you to examine, send, and receive files from other computers over the Internet. Ftp is closely related to telnet in that it allows you to connect directly to a remote computer. However, it is an independent system that facilitates the transfer of files between computers. One way ftp differs from telnet is that you cannot use ftp to run any

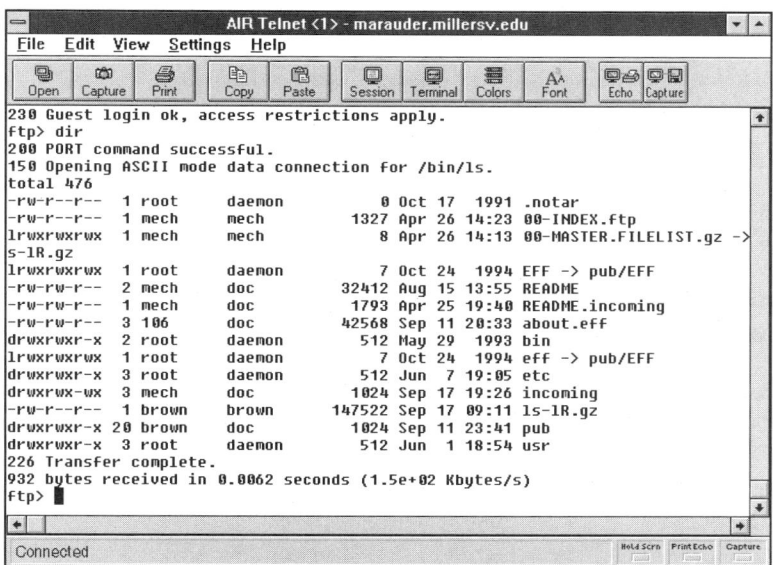

Figure 4-3   A typical listing of files for downloading through ftp from the
Computers and Academic Freedom Archive.

software. It only transfers files. As with telnet you need access to a remote computer to be able to download or retrieve files. However, many ftp sites provide some public access through anonymous ftp.

Anonymous ftp means you may use *anonymous* as your user name. If the ftp site is an anonymous ftp, then you will receive instructions on what password to enter. Typically, the password is guest or your e-mail account name. Most ftp sites severely restrict the number and types of files that are available for downloading and uploading. The reason is simple, an anonymous ftp is open to everyone on the Internet.

A Quick Tour of ftp

As with telnet you must launch ftp either from a menu or as a command. You can access ftp by using the URL address *ftp://ftpaddress*. In many cases, when you execute the ftp command, the ftp> prompt appears. File transfer protocol has a set of commands that control access to files. To access an ftp site, include the site address when invoking ftp. For example, the ftp address *ftp.eff.org* will take you to the Computers and Academic Freedom Archive.

When you seek to download a file, you must first identify the directory where the file resides. This the purpose of the cd command. For example, the command *cd history/us/civilwar* activates *civilwar*, which is a directory of us, which is a directory located in *history*.

After you have located the proper directory, you must know the exact name of the file. Determining the exact name is accomplished by using the dir command. At this point you can download a file with the get command. The command get must be followed by the exact filename and must be case specific. If you issue the get command correctly with the exact filename, the file will be downloaded to your host computer. For example, *get 00-INDEX.ftp* will download the file from *ftp.eff.org*.

ftp Features

Examining Files

In many cases you may want to learn more about the contents of a file before downloading it. To examine an ASCII or text file, you may add the |more command to the end of the get command. For example get 00-INDEX.ftp |more displays the 00-INDEX.ftp file on screen. Information is displayed one screen at a time, and the spacebar is used to scroll to the next screen. Pressing b scrolls up one screen.

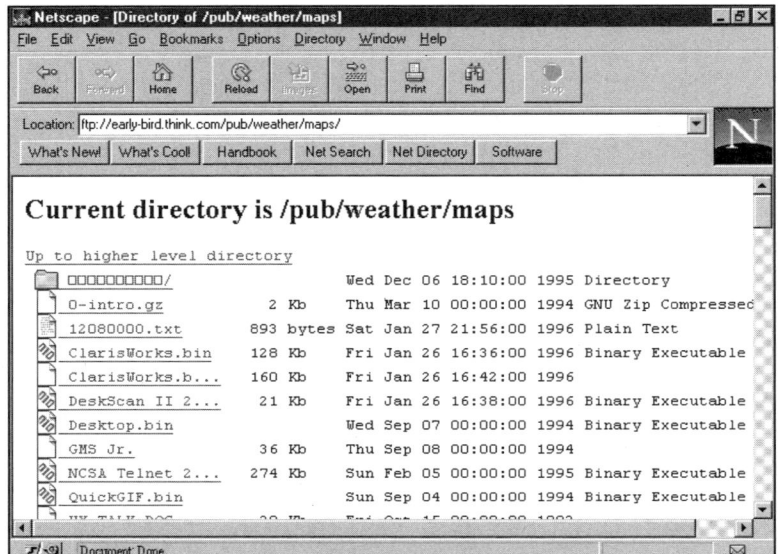

Figure 4-4   You can use an ftp URL to go to various ftp sites in
                      Netscape to download files. To download a file, click on the
                      file name.

New Names

When you download a file, ftp transfers the file and its full filename. This can cause a problem if you intend to use that file on a computer that does not allow lengthy filenames. DOS limits a filename to eight characters. To resolve this problem, you can rename a file as it is downloaded by adding a new filename to the end of the get command. For example, *get document:economic:recovery econ.txt* would send *document:economic: recovery* to your computer as *econ.txt*.

Binary Files

Ftp provides two modes for transferring files — text and binary. In the text mode, only text or ASCII files may be downloaded. In the binary mode, any type of file may be downloaded. Binary files include software, formatted word processing files, and spreadsheet files. Some of the more popular extensions for binary files include .exe, .gif., .bmp, .pcx, .zip, .doc, .wks, and .wpd. This is only a partial list of the common binary or formatted file extensions.

To switch to the binary mode you need to used the binary command. By typing binary, a message appears indicating the type is set to I. Once in this mode, you can use the get command to download any file.

INDEX and README

Many ftp sites provide either INDEX or README files that describe the contents of available files. It is a good idea to use the more parameter at the end of the get command to display the contents of these files.